Welcome to "o· Fun ar Christmas 'Would You ꞁꞋutꞋꞁeꞋ ꞬꞋueꞆtꞋuꞋꞋꞆ ꞉ ꞋꞋꞋꞋu book is designed to add a fun and playful twist to your holiday gatherings. Whether you're hosting a Christmas party, spending time with family and friends, or just looking to inject some humor into the holiday season, this collection of Grinch-themed "Would You Rather" questions is the perfect choice.

Inside these pages, you'll find a wide variety of thought-provoking and entertaining questions that will have everyone laughing, debating, and getting into the festive spirit. Get ready to challenge your guests to make tough choices and share some hearty laughs along the way.

Whether you're a true Grinch aficionado or just looking to spice up your Christmas celebrations, "Would You Rather Christmas Grinch Questions" has something for everyone. So, grab a cozy spot by the fireplace, pour yourself some eggnog, and let the fun begin!

Wishing you a Merry Grinchmas filled with laughter and good times.

fifty

Would you rather

Fifty Would You Rather Questions- Grinch Edition

The holiday season is a time of joy, laughter, and making cherished memories with family and friends. Inspired by the timeless tale of Dr. Seuss's beloved character, the Grinch, this eBook offers a delightful twist to the classic game of "Would You Rather."

In this Grinch Edition, we invite you to embark on a whimsical journey through the whimsical world of Whoville and the Grinch's cave, exploring the holiday spirit in a unique and playful way. Whether you're a fan of the mischievous Grinch or the heartwarming Whos, these 50 carefully crafted "Would You Rather" questions are designed to bring a touch of Grinchy charm and festive cheer to your holiday gatherings.

Inside these digital pages, you'll find a delightful collection of questions that challenge your imagination, tickle your funny bone, and inspire thoughtful reflection. Would you rather help the Grinch steal Christmas presents or join the Whos in their joyful celebrations? Would you rather have the Grinch's ability to be grumpy and cynical or the Whos' ability to be cheerful and optimistic? These questions, inspired by the Grinch's escapades and the Whos' unwavering holiday spirit, are sure to spark lively discussions and bring smiles to faces young and old.

So, gather your family and friends, cozy up by the fireplace, and dive into the whimsical world of Whoville with these Grinch-inspired "Would You Rather" questions. May your holiday season be filled with laughter, love, and the spirit of togetherness, just like the heartwarming story of the Grinch and the Whos. Let the festivities begin!

How To Use

This eBook is designed to bring a touch of holiday magic and a sprinkle of Grinchy mischief to your gatherings. Whether you're hosting a family game night, a holiday party, or simply spending quality time with friends, these Grinch-inspired "Would You Rather" questions are the perfect addition to your festive celebrations. Here's how you can make the most of this eBook:

- Choose Your Setting: Decide on the perfect moment to introduce these Grinchy questions. Whether it's during a holiday dinner, a cozy night in, or a lively party, these questions are sure to entertain and engage your guests.
- Gather Your Audience: Bring together your family, friends, or colleagues and create a circle where everyone can participate. The more diverse the group, the more entertaining the responses are likely to be.
- Read Aloud: As the host, take turns reading the Grinch-themed "Would You Rather" questions out loud. Encourage participants to listen carefully and visualize the whimsical scenarios presented in each question.
- Encourage Discussions: After each question, encourage participants to share their answers and reasoning behind their choices. Some questions might lead to laughter, while others might spark intriguing debates— either way, it's all part of the fun!
- Embrace Creativity: Don't be afraid to let your imagination run wild! Some questions might have unexpected or humorous outcomes. Feel free to explore creative responses and enjoy the imaginative and festive atmosphere.
- Rotate Roles: Encourage different participants to take turns reading the questions. This keeps the game dynamic and ensures everyone gets a chance to contribute to the fun.
- Enjoy the Grinchy Spirit: Remember, the primary goal is to have fun and enjoy the holiday spirit with your loved ones. Embrace the Grinchy charm and let the laughter and merriment fill the room.
- Share and Reflect: As the game progresses, take moments to reflect on the heartwarming themes of the Grinch story. Discuss how the Grinch's transformation and the Whos' kindness can inspire us all during the holiday season and beyond.

So, without further ado, let the Grinch-themed "Would You Rather" game begin! May your celebrations be filled with joy, laughter, and the spirit of togetherness, just like the heartwarming story of the Grinch and the Whos. Enjoy!

Would You Rather:

Would you rather steal all the presents
OR
all the Christmas decorations in Whoville?

Would You Rather:

Would you rather have Max the dog
OR
Cindy Lou Who as your sidekick?

Would You Rather:

Would you rather live in a cave on
Mount Crumpit
OR
in a cozy house in Whoville?

Would You Rather:

Would you rather have a heart that's
two sizes too small
OR
a head full of schemes?

Would You Rather:

Would you rather have your heart
grow three sizes in one day
OR
your Grinchy attitude last forever?

Would You Rather:

Would you rather eat roast beast for
every meal
OR
survive on a diet of only green
vegetables?

Would you rather have your sled
loaded with presents
OR
your heart filled with the joy of giving?

Would you rather be stuck in Whoville
forever
OR
live in isolation on Mount Crumpit?

Would You Rather:

Would you rather have your heart
warmed by the Whos' kindness
OR
stay cold-hearted forever?

Would You Rather:

Would you rather have your Grinchy
plans always succeed
OR
learn the true meaning of Christmas?

Would You Rather:

Would you rather have your Grinchy grin
OR
a genuine smile from the bottom of your heart?

Would You Rather:

Would you rather be known as the Grinch
OR
have a different identity altogether?

Would you rather have your heart
melted by a heartfelt song
OR
remain immune to music's magic?

Would you rather have your heart
stolen by love
OR
guard it against all feelings?

Have a family pet
OR
not?

Would you rather be surrounded by
Whos singing carols
OR
live in a silent, Grinchy world?

Would you rather have a Grinchy
sense of humor
OR
appreciate the Whos' lighthearted
jokes?

Would You Rather:

Would you rather have the strength of
ten Grinches
OR
the wisdom of a thousand Whos?

Would You Rather:

Would you rather have a heartwarming
reunion with your family
OR
continue your solitary Grinchy life?

Would You Rather:

Would you rather have a snowball
fight with the Whos
OR
enjoy a peaceful day by yourself?

Would you rather have the
Grinchmobile
OR
a magical flying sleigh like Santa's?

Would you rather have a Grinchy dance-
off
OR
watch the Whos perform a heartwarming
dance?

Would you rather be best friends with
Cindy Lou Who
OR
have an alliance with the Grinch's loyal
dog, Max?

Would you rather have a Grinchy green
complexion
OR
a natural, rosy Whoville glow?

Would you rather have your heart grow
three sizes every Christmas
OR
have a permanently Grinch-sized heart?

Would you rather have a snowball
fight with the Whos
OR
participate in their festive feast?

Would You Rather:

Would you rather have the Grinch's wit and cleverness
OR
the Whos' kindness and compassion?

Would You Rather:

Would you rather be surrounded by Christmas lights
OR
live in eternal darkness on Mount Crumpit?

Would you rather have a Grinchy
sense of style
OR
the Whos' fashionable taste in
clothing?

Would you rather have a Grinchy attitude and
lots of material possessions
OR
be poor but surrounded by loving friends and
family?

Would You Rather:

Would you rather be transformed into a
Who for a day
OR
have a Who experience being the Grinch?

Would You Rather:

Have a family vacation to Disney
World
OR
Universal Studios?

Would you rather have a Grinchy singing voice
OR
the ability to appreciate the Whos' melodious tunes?

Would you rather have a snowball fight with the Whos
OR
share a cup of hot cocoa with them?

Would You Rather:

Would you rather have the Grinch's
ability to steal Christmas
OR
the Whos' ability to spread joy and
cheer?

Would You Rather:

Would you rather have a Grinchy green thumb &
grow only prickly, unappealing plants
OR
have a magical garden full of beautiful, blooming
flowers like in Whoville?

Would You Rather:

Would you rather have your heart
warmed by the Whos' caroling
OR
stay immune to the power of music?

Would You Rather:

Would you rather have a Grinchy
sense of humor
OR
laugh wholeheartedly like the Whos?

Would you rather have the Grinch's icy glare
OR
he Whos' warm, inviting smiles?

Would you rather have a Grinchy feast of unappetizing food
OR
enjoy a delightful meal cooked by the Whos?

Would you rather have your heart
stolen by a charming Who
OR
remain unswayed by love?

Would you rather have the Grinch's
cunning
OR
the Whos' innocence?

Would you rather have a Grinchy snowball fight
OR
build snowmen with the Whos?

Would you rather have a Grinchy heart
that's always cold
OR
a heart that can be warmed by the
Whos' kindness?

Would you rather have the Grinch's
ability to scheme
OR
the Whos' ability to forgive and forget?

Would You Rather:

Would you rather have your heart
touched by the Whos' generosity
OR
remain indifferent to their acts of
kindness?

Would You Rather:

Would you rather have a Grinchy
sense of smell
OR
appreciate the delightful scents of
Christmas in Whoville?

Would You Rather:

Would you rather have a Grinchy feast
of strange and unappetizing foods
OR
enjoy a traditional Whoville holiday
meal?

Would you rather have a Grinchy
sense of fashion
OR
the Whos' impeccable style?

Would you rather have a Grinchy green
complexion that glows
OR
the natural radiance of a contented
Who?

Would You Rather:

Would you rather have the Grinch's Grinchy attitude
OR
embrace the warmth and love of the Whos?

Made in the USA
Monee, IL
10 December 2024

73024090R00017